Getting it Paid

A Bill-Paying Planner and Organizer

Flash Planners and Notebooks

Flash Planners and Notebooks

JOURNALS & NOTEBOOKS

Copyright 2016

Due Date	Expenses	Amount	Paid

Month of:

Notes:

Food	
Water	
Electricity	
House Rental	
Others	
Total	

Due Date	Expenses	Amount	Paid

Month of:
Notes:

Food

Water

Electricity

House Rental

Others

Total

Due Date	Expenses	Amount	Paid

Month of:
Notes:

Food
Water
Electricity
House Rental
Others
Total

Due Date	Expenses	Amount	Paid

Month of:
Notes:

Food

Water

Electricity

House Rental

Others

Total

Due Date	Expenses	Amount	Paid

Month of:
Notes:

Food
Water
Electricity
House Rental
Others
Total

Due Date	Expenses	Amount	Paid

Month of:
Notes:

Food

Water

Electricity

House Rental

Others

Total

Due Date	Expenses	Amount	Paid

Month of:

Notes:

Food

Water

Electricity

House Rental

Others

Total

Due Date	Expenses	Amount	Paid

Month of:
Notes:

Food
Water
Electricity
House Rental
Others
Total

Due Date	Expenses	Amount	Paid

Month of:
Notes:

Food

Water

Electricity

House Rental

Others

Total

Due Date	Expenses	Amount	Paid

Month of:
Notes:

Food
Water
Electricity
House Rental
Others
Total

Due Date	Expenses	Amount	Paid

Month of:
Notes:

Food
Water
Electricity
House Rental
Others
Total

Due Date	Expenses	Amount	Paid

Month of:
Notes:

Food

Water

Electricity

House Rental

Others

Total

Due Date	Expenses	Amount	Paid

Month of:

Notes:

Food
Water
Electricity
House Rental
Others
Total

Due Date	Expenses	Amount	Paid

Month of:
Notes:

Food

Water

Electricity

House Rental

Others

Total

Due Date	Expenses	Amount	Paid

Month of:
Notes:

Food
Water
Electricity
House Rental
Others
Total

Due Date	Expenses	Amount	Paid

Month of:
Notes:

Food	
Water	
Electricity	
House Rental	
Others	
Total	

Due Date	Expenses	Amount	Paid

Month of:
Notes:

Food

Water

Electricity

House Rental

Others

Total

Due Date	Expenses	Amount	Paid

Month of:
Notes:

Food
Water
Electricity
House Rental
Others
Total

Due Date	Expenses	Amount	Paid

Month of:
Notes:

Food
Water
Electricity
House Rental
Others
Total

Due Date	Expenses	Amount	Paid

Month of:
Notes:

Food

Water

Electricity

House Rental

Others

Total

Due Date	Expenses	Amount	Paid

Month of:

Notes:

Food
Water
Electricity
House Rental
Others
Total

Due Date	Expenses	Amount	Paid

Month of:
Notes:

Food	
Water	
Electricity	
House Rental	
Others	
Total	

Due Date	Expenses	Amount	Paid

Month of:
Notes:

Food
Water
Electricity
House Rental
Others
Total

Due Date	Expenses	Amount	Paid

Month of:
Notes:

Food

Water

Electricity

House Rental

Others

Total

Due Date	Expenses	Amount	Paid

Month of:
Notes:

Food	
Water	
Electricity	
House Rental	
Others	
Total	

Due Date	Expenses	Amount	Paid

Month of:
Notes:

Food	
Water	
Electricity	
House Rental	
Others	
Total	

Due Date	Expenses	Amount	Paid

Month of:
Notes:

Food	
Water	
Electricity	
House Rental	
Others	
Total	

Due Date	Expenses	Amount	Paid

Month of:
Notes:

Food	
Water	
Electricity	
House Rental	
Others	
Total	

Due Date	Expenses	Amount	Paid

Month of:
Notes:

Food

Water

Electricity

House Rental

Others

Total

Due Date	Expenses	Amount	Paid

Month of:

Notes:

Food
Water
Electricity
House Rental
Others
Total

Due Date	Expenses	Amount	Paid

Month of:
Notes:

Food
Water
Electricity
House Rental
Others
Total

Due Date	Expenses	Amount	Paid

Month of:
Notes:

Food

Water

Electricity

House Rental

Others

Total

Due Date	Expenses	Amount	Paid

Month of:
Notes:

Food
Water
Electricity
House Rental
Others
Total

Due Date	Expenses	Amount	Paid

Month of:
Notes:

Food

Water

Electricity

House Rental

Others

Total

Due Date	Expenses	Amount	Paid

Month of:
Notes:

Food
Water
Electricity
House Rental
Others
Total

Due Date	Expenses	Amount	Paid

Month of:
Notes:

Food
Water
Electricity
House Rental
Others
Total

Due Date	Expenses	Amount	Paid

Month of:
Notes:

Food
Water
Electricity
House Rental
Others
Total

Due Date	Expenses	Amount	Paid

Month of:

Notes:

Food

Water

Electricity

House Rental

Others

Total

Due Date	Expenses	Amount	Paid

Month of:
Notes:

Food
Water
Electricity
House Rental
Others
Total

Due Date	Expenses	Amount	Paid

Month of:
Notes:

Food
Water
Electricity
House Rental
Others
Total

Due Date	Expenses	Amount	Paid

Month of:
Notes:

Food
Water
Electricity
House Rental
Others
Total

Due Date	Expenses	Amount	Paid

Month of:
Notes:

Food
Water
Electricity
House Rental
Others
Total

Due Date	Expenses	Amount	Paid

Month of:
Notes:

Food
Water
Electricity
House Rental
Others
Total

Due Date	Expenses	Amount	Paid

Month of:
Notes:

Food

Water

Electricity

House Rental

Others

Total

Due Date	Expenses	Amount	Paid

Month of:

Notes:

Food
Water
Electricity
House Rental
Others
Total

Due Date	Expenses	Amount	Paid

Month of:

Notes:

Food
Water
Electricity
House Rental
Others
Total

Due Date	Expenses	Amount	Paid

Month of:
Notes:

Food
Water
Electricity
House Rental
Others
Total

Due Date	Expenses	Amount	Paid

Month of:
Notes:

Food

Water

Electricity

House Rental

Others

Total

Due Date	Expenses	Amount	Paid

Month of:
Notes:

Food

Water

Electricity

House Rental

Others

Total